TRANSDUCER

TRANS

DUCER

Jeanne Heuving

chax press 2008

Acknowledgements:
The following poems have appeared in these journals: "Leafy," "Berry Mouth," "Killing Ants," "Shining Power," "Divided Lights," "Jewelry," and "Furrow" in *Titanic Operas;* "Fortunate Torsos," "Fine Reticule," "Grays," and "Drowse" in 26; "Brows," "Dowse," "Rhododendron," and "Travel Waves" in *Bird Dog;* "Arrowwood" and "Sea Lily" in *Subtext Annual 2002;* "Florescence" in *Volt;* and "Limbing" and "Limning" in *First Intensity.* Reprints: "Fortunate Torsos," "Fine Reticule," "Brows," "Grays," "Drowse," "Dowse," and "Furrow" in *'A Right Good Salvo of Barks': Critics and Poets on Marianne Moore.*

ISBN 978-0925904-70-6
Chax Press / 650 E. 9th St. / Tucson AZ 85705-8584 / USA

The light foot hears you and the brightness begins

— Robert Duncan, *A Poem Beginning with a Line by Pindar*

FREQUENCY

The magical resonance of transfer becomes extinct through the issue of coin.

— after J.H. Prynne

LEAFY

Berries glistening
Piled to
The rafters
Popping bird
At window
Sprig in beak

BERRY MOUTH

Red casting lips
Small torn flesh
On teeth, tongue
Seeds throughout
Mouth pricking
Gums

KILLING ANTS

Rolling
Between thumb
And forefinger
And still the
Lithe body
Twists
Uncertain whether
This wiry filigree
Is dead
Or alive
Black outer
Gold inner

SHINING POWER

Bird diving
Into sliding
Door
Finger into beak
Pulls out berry
Clean as
A whistle
Muscles holding
Thorax relax
Preens
Shining
Power

DIVIDED LIGHTS

The house
A truck
Careening
Two windows
Beaming the
Blown apart
World
A cat in
Each window
Watching
The moving
Breathing
Alive

JEWELRY

Edged
Wrapped
Cinched
Crinkled
Latched
Fastened
Harvester
Ant
Wheat
Berry
Blood
Stone

FORTUNATE TORSOS

Something like me. Dirty water in the quart jar we tried to keep clean. Slosh with boats of bark, slur into currents. Three plastic daisies on astroturf. Nothing strikes like a hawk, a crouching hare. She sings her rose petal body home. To rinse until the clear whitens. Angle eyes. Sweetheart.

FINE RETICULE

To say any such thing that will make us glad. Rub a dub dub three men in a tub. Three plastic daisies on astroturf. Entangling strands of dirty water. To clean until the clear whitens. Pitches salt. Sheep roam in the gloaming.

BROWS

Mouth around mouth around words. Mouthing words. Soft shoe. Shoeing it. Schussing down the mountain. Sluice run off. Such unnatural preternatural clarity. Rough brown roads visible from this far distance. Lofty. Rafter. Browse.

GRAYS

A lemon snow cone. Sluice run off. Fine screen catching stones, some pretty. Tiny craniums, blackened skulls. Black netting crawling over eyes. Beauty mark. A valve or gate to regulate the flow. To flood or drench with released water. To draw off. Sidelong. Graze.

DROWSE

Berries. Black dot. Glistening. Piled to the rafters. Popping bird. Toppling trees. Twig in beak. Beaking it. B-eking it. Clattering capsules. Broken chamois. Bare branched mountain ash with clusters of orange-red. Smashed on sidewalk. Smeared yellow. Dowse.

DOWSE

Drenched weave. Reordering to get the snap of synapse. Lines on cerebral cortex. Lines inside fleshy creases creasing secreting lemony watery. Berry juice on lips. Berry flesh on tongue. Douse.

Flora

It is important to understand the concept of bandwidth, or range of frequencies, of a transducer.

— *Characteristics of Transducers*

Travel

Waves

salty
sea water

stars in eyes
hair stranded
clumped

white on hair
whet on face

patch of light
breaking

Travel

Waves

coating

germinate
implant

glossy
lips

maidenhead
silkening

Travel

Waves

reeds

hollow

concentric

minnows

stipple

ripple

glisten

Travel

Waves

penstemons
capsules
spill

persimmons
fleshy
white

glister

marred

stint of petals

meager

wet rose

leaf

See H.D.'s Sea Garden

spare

prostrate

crying

blossoms

green sheaths

See H.D.'s Sea Garden

Flora

And the wave runs in the beach groove

And the wave runs in the beech groove

Grapes with no seed but sea foam

See Pound's Sea Cantos

Arrowwood

viburnum

nodules

honey blisters

cottony seed

tick

mite

Rhodendron

guelden rose

markings on petal

like an umlaat

itch of sex

rehearsal

form

Sword Lily

lancing leaves

glancing water

dewey sheen

glans

ocellus

seedum

Sea Plume

milty

silty

into mouth

through side

Plaster of Paris

Scotch Tape

CHTHONIC

The first step in the Eleusinian mysteries had to do with sex.

— H.D., *Notes on Thought and Vision*

A COLUMN OF ANTS

Set down softly
In a retreat strewn
With roses and rose stems

Bell-shaped flowers
Foam flowers
Small compressed pellets

A rill glistening with glassy
Waters, breezes furrowing
Flumes

Channels of bed covers
Creasing with winds
And shadows

Taking out the lamp
Disgorging a drop of oil
From the tip of the flame

Scorching his shoulder
Rolling into feathers
Runnels

Bows and arrows, quiver
Tangled in a heap
At the foot of the bed

A neglected assortment
Of harvesting equipment
Sickles, scythes

Seeds blown into her eyes
A pelting storm
A halcyon season

Of small white stuffs
Dry chaff, which
She cannot decipher

A column of ants
Wave after wave
Of the sespedalian tribe

Sorts them into piles of
Wheat, barley, millet
Chickpeas, lentils, beans

Gathering soft gold

Eyes shining as coins

WELL OF FLOWERS

Because a flowering from the depths

was thought to take place there

Takes the entire pomegranate into his mouth

spits out seeds one at a time

A honey sweet seed grazes her lips

keeps her starving

Flashes his blue eyes at her

frozen corn flowers

Branches extending down into the axils

of the leafy stem

Black seeds spilling

FURROW

How all is a fertile field ever threatening
Plowed too close like an ominous sky
Earth ever opened the possibility of
Into the plowed furrowed lined earth
A fertile plow into the staid forestation
Into the silvered peat moss lined with
A jewelry box felted with diamonds

---

seeds with their hooded black jackets
carapace of insect left to wither in the wind
to mash with a mallet to get the insides out
a round hole bored in the seed by a weevil
seeds of the penstemons and the mulleins
are easy to remove by the crushing method
to remove the seed heads the cones must be
split open washed inside minute stuffs

the possibility of light falling onto his face
the possibility of walking into a sunlit alcove
the sunlit alcove fitting rippling like a glove
the glove moving from finger tip to forearm
silky on flesh receptive to being touched
harvested when a light brown will turn black
deadening hollow black seeds refusing

What does not go away this
Mascared eyes, Cleopatra
Charcoaled Marlene Dietrich
Wanting at the grave as it
Leaks light

FLORESCENCE

Through hallways of rising water
Dark sedge to stay here in this
Netherworld refusing to see above
A water line as it creases the eye
Swimming forward to this line
Of entry no entry you hold me
Rising descent into nearness
To see through other eyes
To see through mine
The plunging water picks me up
This lunging of a place
Moving forward into
Underwater under kind
Traveling dark stream of streaked
Beatitude choosing to eat the seeds
Of death to take in each grain
Winnowing for grain for seed
Heated by sun flooding hallway

By river watching through mirror
Filtered, carrying sludge, sedge
Underwater coursing vision
Line of water as it cuts

LIMNING

Psyche was to inherit all, on one condition that she not seek to see her Eros in the light.

— Robert Duncan, *The H.D. Book*

LIMNING

The possibility in this clutch
That I should find you.
And still you are traveling
Long lane with trees
Slashed hello.

To see your face anywhere.
Soft pulp of body.
Untold reflection makes cuts
In skin. Struck tine.
Reparative. Cut.

Please comply with lighted signs.
Direct passage away from aircraft.
White hyphenated line. Floatable cushion.
Brace position.
Hug.

Trying to find you in clutch.
Branching to fall. Used tire dump.
Harvester junk yard. Too random
Finally. No sound issues
For a pass key to the frame.

Long dark shafts of storm
Supplanting love. Children's
Dark eyes lost in
Childhood's recesses.
Vacating the capitol

As the storm of winter approaches
Sky whitening, slackening.
Going into you as we depart
Spilled nectarine
Dash of cinnamon.

Being lost in a hotel.
Candleabras, catacombs
Candle behind eyes as we
Journey through shadowy
Brown cavernous mountains

When all that rings
The horizon are trees.
Tears pummeled out of the earth.
This pummeling of our
Bodies ever to go away.

To sear seer. This going around
Emptiness. How we both form
In the upwelling of your drifting
Sage.
Salver.

Stille nacht. Stillness into balance.
This tipping into each other, into eyes.
This preening of your flesh.
Sorrow of your sorrow
Black gold.

Denatured neuter.
Fearsome sans toothed pines
Hoarfrost standing in for appetite.
This pellucid showering
In the gesture of comeliness.

Endless night with you, in you.
Pitch of pented paint. Feint going over.
This ever surfacing, breaking
Scuttle sky hawks
Wheeling doves

Eagles next
Satyr
Dog.
Keyless exchange of no entry.
Your body an empty rack

Of nerveless intent
Where feeling might begin.
Drearest loss of spell.
Syncopate. Double intake
Breath.

Love long lost discovering.
Sudden dusk of light
Agog with overcry.
Never more.
Never the less.

This writing in your wake. To return
With infinite regress of *stille nacht* blue.
Windowless agape. Eros dark night
Of winter storm. This whitest
Darkest gem.

Itinerant traveler over the rust belt.
Fradulent eyes. Hands.
Watershed.
This always to begin in me.
Decibel. Siecle.

This coming into and out of me.
Foreign body of the *arriviste*
Onto new soil.
Fallen blackened leaves.
Telescopic syncopating

Into never ever more could we.
Rind of orange dropped soundlessly
Glassed in hallways, passageways
Thorax opening, promulgating.
Lax.

Falling in between each other
Into face, coinage, minted
Wheeling, grayed wants.
Keyless exchange
Of no entry.

Thunder whitening breath
Boisterous no sight
As the storm of winter approaches
Promises to blanket
An entire region.

Pellucid translucent rice
Eaten with termites, tics
Sticks in cotton.
A dark swirling comma
Reaching down.

Dear, drearest, moody blue
Veined, silvered tip of quill
Till dark keep writing into
The no appearance
Of disappearance.

Folding into ewes, eyes
Sheer joy falling, this tuck
In myself, into the hourglass
Crystals sifting
Over the world.

LIMBING

How to inhabit setting its sails
its valences in shrouds so that
one lapses. Limning. Limbing.
Entering me, looking out my eyes,
biting lips.
At the fourth watch he came
to them, walking on the sea.
But when they saw him moving
there, they were terrified, saying
'It is a ghost!' And moaned in fear.
Lobster pincers pinching. This
forward moving froward. Frown.

Body held in transport
over rippling waters, wavy lines
on a monitor screen.
This long slow carrying as a bride
over a threshold. Seeds in eyes
hair and mouth, mashing them
with tip of tongue into a mealy pulp
pushing it into all corners of mouth.
And a great storm of wind arose
and the waves beat into the boat
so that the boat was already filling.
And he woke and rebuked the wind
And said to the sea, 'Peace.'
A breaking that multiplies. Flask.

That could only come from
these fleshless nights. Landlocked
pressed into the hold. Ribbed curvature
battened wood.
He went with them to a place
called Gethsemane.
'My soul is sorrowful, even to death.
Remain here and watch with me.'
Pungent olive.
White bark.
Stripling.

How could a key, key this,
when a key is a prehensile.
Insert into me and my body
will talk, one-thousand petalled lily.
Uvula. Vulva.
Enfold. Enclose.
Mary took a pound of pure nard
and anointed his feet
and wiped his feet with her hair,
and the house was filled with fragrance.
Filling the gap.

Tracing where the rope has been. Incinerate
desire. Into the steaming garden
of broken stalks. I lean into
your body as into a shadow,
spear of grass. *Supposing him to be*
the gardener. Rabboni. A slit.
Put your finger here and see my hands,
put out your hand and place it in my side.
One of the soldiers pierced his side
with a spear, and at once there came out
blood and water. Deep set eyes.
I draw you to me a line of verse
unfeeling where you are breathing still.

SOURCES

Characteristics of Transducers can be found at www.ndt~edu.org.

In "A Column of Ants," the lines "Disgorging a drop of oil / From the tip of the flame" and "Wave after Wave / Of the sespedalian tribe" are from Apuleius' *The Golden Ass*, as translated by P.G. Walsh, Oxford University Press, 1994.

In "Furrow," the second section is indebted to Harry R. Phillips' *Growing and Propagating Wild Flowers*, University of North Carolina Press, 1985.

In "Limning," the lines "Reflections make / cuts in the skin" and "No sound issues for a pass key to the frame" are adapted from J.H. Prynne.

Otherwise sources are indicated in the poems.

Chax Press programs and publications are supported by donations from individuals and foundations, as well as from the Tucson Pima Arts Council and the Arizona Commission on the Arts, with funding from the State of Arizona and the National Endowment for the Arts.

Arizona Commission on the Arts

NATIONAL ENDOWMENT FOR THE ARTS

A great nation deserves great art.

TUCSON PIMA ARTS COUNCIL

Some Recent and Forthcoming Books from Chax Press

Fiction

Hilton Obenzinger, *Busy Dying*
Kass Fleisher, *Accidental Species*

Poetry

John Tritica, *Sound Remains*
Elizabeth Treadwell, *Wardolly*
Karen Mac Cormack, *Implexures II*
Steve McCaffery, *Slightly Left of Thinking*
Michael Cross, *In Felt Treeling*
Bruce Andrews, *Swoon Noir*
Tim Peterson, *Since I Moved In*
Paul Naylor, *Arranging Nature*
Sarah Riggs, *Waterwork*
Glen Mott, *Analects on a Chinese Screen*
Charles Borkhuis, *Afterimage*
Beth Joselow, *Begin At Once*
Linh Dinh, *Jam Alerts*
Linda Russo, *Mirth*
Joe Amato, *Under Virga*

Artist's Book Editions/Book Arts Works

Kathleen Fraser and Nancy Tokar Miller, *Witness*

More books, and more information about Chax Press, appear on our web site: http://chax.org.